We Are All Different

Rebecca Rissman

Heinemann
LIBRARY

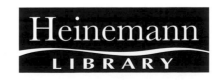

H www.heinemannlibrary.co.uk
Visit our website to find out more information about Heinemann Library books.

To order:
☎ Phone 44 (0) 1865 888066
📄 Send a fax to 44 (0) 1865 314091
💻 Visit the Heinemann Bookshop at www.heinemannlibrary.co.uk to browse our catalogue and order online.

Heinemann Library is an imprint of Capstone Global Library Limited, a company incorporated in England and Wales having its registered office at 7 Pilgrim Street, London, EC4V 6LB – Registered company number: 6695582

Heinemann is a registered trademark of Pearson Education Limited, under licence to Capstone Global Library Limited

Text © Capstone Global Library Limited 2009
First published in hardback in 2009
The moral rights of the proprietor have been asserted.

Edited by Rebecca Rissman, Charlotte Guillain and Catherine Veitch
Designed by Joanna Hinton-Malivoire
Picture research by Tracy Cummins
Production by Duncan Gilbert
Originated by Dot Gradations Ltd
Printed and bound in China by South China Printing Company Ltd

ISBN 978 0 431 19302 1 (hardback)
13 12 11 10 09
10 9 8 7 6 5 4 3 2 1

British Library Cataloguing in Publication Data
Rissman, Rebecca
We are all different. - (Acorn plus)
1. Anthropology - Juvenile literature 2. Persons - Juvenile literature
301
A full catalogue record for this book is available from the British Library.

Acknowledgements
We would like to thank the following for permission to reproduce photographs:
©Alamy pp. **6L** (Blaine Harrington III), **17R** (moodboard); ©AP Images p. **19L** (TYLER MALLORY); ©Corbis pp. **4** (Chuck Savage), **11TR** (Markus Moellenberg), **16** (Ed Kashi); ©drr.net pp. **14** (Brett Snow), **18** (enzodalverme.com); ©Getty Images pp. **5** (Mike Powell), **6R** (John W. Banagan), **12** (Mike Powell), **17L** (John Rowley), **20** (Jack Hollingsworth), **21** (Steve Satushek); ©istockphoto pp. **6M** (Maria Bibikova), **13BR** (Luís Graça); ©Jupiter Images p. **13TR** (Thinkstock); ©Shutterstock p. **7L** (David Garry); ©Peter Arnold p. **15R** (sinopictures); ©Shutterstck pp. **7M** (Douglas Freer), **7R** (Max Earey), **8BR** (WizData, inc), **9R** (Diana Lundin), **11L** (Supri Suharjoto), **11BR** (Alistair Scott), **13L** (Andresr), **15L** (Anita Patterson Peppers), **19R** (Niamh Baldock); ©Superstock p. **10** (Corbis/Royalty Free); ©The World Bank pp. **8L** (Bill Lyons), **8TR** (Eric Miller), **9M** (Eric Miller), **9L** (Trevor Samson).

Cover photograph of a group of people reproduced with permission of ©Agefotostock (John Birdsall Social Issues). Back cover photograph of children in a playground reproduced with permission of ©Superstock (Corbis/Royalty Free).

Every effort has been made to contact copyright holders of material reproduced in this book. Any omissions will be rectified in subsequent printings if notice is given to the publishers.

Disclaimer
All the Internet addresses (URLs) given in this book were valid at the time of going to press. However, due to the dynamic nature of the Internet, some addresses may have changed, or sites may have changed or ceased to exist since publication. While the author and Publishers regret any inconvenience this may cause readers, no responsibility for any such changes can be accepted by either the author or the Publishers.

Contents

Some words are shown in bold, **like this.** They are explained in “Words to know” on page 23.

Differences

We are all different ages and sizes. We all have different coloured hair and skin. We are all good at different things. What differences can you see?

We are all special. Our differences make us special.

People live in different countries. Some people's family may have lived in another country. Some people move to live in a new country. What country do you live in?

People live in different homes. Some people live in houses. Some people live in flats. What type of home do you live in?

People go to different schools. Some people wear a school uniform. Some people use computers at school. Some people learn outdoors and some learn in a classroom.

People go to different jobs. Some people work with a computer and others work with their hands. Some people have jobs that help us, such as doctors, teachers, and fire fighters.

Playing

People play in different ways. There are many different ways to have fun. People can play inside and outside.

Some people play computer games. Some people play music. Some people play sport.

Moving

People move in different ways. People move for different reasons.

Some people move to play. Some people move to stay fit and healthy. Some people move to get to places. Some people use a **wheelchair** to help them move.

Reading

There are many different ways to read. We can read books, magazines, newspapers, signs, computers, and many other things.

Some people read with their eyes. Some people read **Braille** with their fingertips.

Learning

People learn in different ways. There are different ways to **understand**.

Some children learn at home with their parents. Some children learn at school with a teacher.

Communicating

People talk in different ways. People listen in different ways. There are many different ways to **communicate**.

Some people communicate with their hands, using **sign language**. Some people communicate with their voices. We can even communicate with our faces.

Respect

Everyone is different. It is important to **respect** the differences of others.

Our differences make us special!

How are you different?

How do you play?

How do you move?

How do you read?

How do you learn?

How do you communicate?

Words to know

Braille	system of raised bumps that people can read with their fingers. People with visual impairments can use Braille.
communicate	to share thoughts, feelings, or facts with others
respect	to show that something or someone is important
sign language	way to communicate using hand signals for letters or words
understand	to know or learn
wheelchair	chair with wheels. Some people use a wheelchair to get around.

Index

Note to parents and teachers

Before reading

Explain to children that people can be both different and alike. Discuss how all people are unique and special, but that we can have things in common, too. Assist the class in making a list of things that all the children have in common (e.g. "We live in Manchester," or "We learn maths"). Write these things on the board for the children to see.

After reading

Ask children to write a list of adjectives about themselves. Then, ask the children to swap lists with another child to see if they used any of the same adjectives.